Journey Workbook
The Road Map to Business Success

Printed in the Unites States of America

Cover Designer: Visions Made Plain LLC.
Book Editor: Tamika L. Sims

ISBN 978-0-9992902-0-0

The Road Map Workbook

Table of Contents:

Acknowledgements

I want to first thank God for birthing the vision.

My Husband Houston Harris for being so understanding while working long hours, your love, and support.

My daughter Hannah Joy Harris for your good behavior while mommy worked late nights and for being my biggest motivation.

My business partner Daryn Murphy for all your hardwork and dedication to see this project through.

Joy McLaughlin-Harris

I would like to thank God for planting these seeds, giving the wisdom, and the concepts for this book.

My wife Judy Murphy for always being there to support my dreams and visions no matter how big they get.

My boys Dorayn, Josiah, & Bryson for challenging me to keep dreaming. When I get tired I look in your faces and keep pushing.

My business partner Joy McLaughlin-Harris for agreeing to take this journey with me it was divine. This was a perfect fit and I look forward to the next project.

Daryn Murphy

Forward

When I think of a road map, I think of the maps I pick up from the rest stop with a sheet I unfold with roads and interstates to assist me in getting from one place to another. It can sometimes look difficult to understand, but when I take a little time to dissect the map's flow, It's a little easier, but there are still challenges or unknown things that may happen along the way. This workbook is designed to help you on the road map to business ownership. Let's unfold it now.
-Joy McLaughlin-Harris

When I think of a roadmap, I automatically think of something I need to assist me to get to a destination. I agree that there are challenges with understanding a road map at first. As it is with most things at first glance, but then I take the time to study the map so that I can understand the best way to position myself or maneuver to my desired finish line. You will find out the best way to position and maneuver your business in today's world.
-Daryn Murphy

Notes From Give Them The Business Podcast Episode #1

Exit 1 Examining the Map
Section 1

Brainstorm time: The What, When, How, and Why of your business.

What does your business offer? (products, services)

_____
_____
_____
_____
_____
_____
_____

What is the objective of your business?

_____
_____
_____
_____
_____
_____
_____

What is the startup cost of a business like this and why?

_____
_____
_____
_____
_____
_____

When will you launch your business?

_____
_____
_____
_____

Exit 1 Examining the Map

Section 1

How will you fund it? (Savings, investment, loans, retirement)

_____
_____
_____
_____
_____
_____

When & how are you going to save or raise funds for this business?
List all the details

_____
_____
_____
_____
_____
_____
_____

Why now versus later? Or why later versus now?

_____
_____
_____
_____
_____
_____

What is your why?

_____
_____
_____
_____
_____
_____

Points To Ponder:

"The road to success and the road failure are almost exactly the same"

-Colin A. Davis

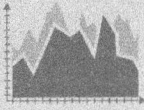

IDEAS RESEARCH STRATEGY TEAMWORK

Exit 1 Examining the Map
Section 1
Timeline for your Journey: How long to go -from idea to startup?

Your business model, industry, and complexity can determine how long it takes to go from an idea to startup. For example, a home-based business could start 10 times faster than a brick and mortar business. For the example below, let's use a franchise or home-based business built with no employees or a product productions company that could startup within a couple of months. A service or retail business could open six to 12 months if researched well and you find great suppliers early on. It also helps if you are a "people person" or can tap into an existing network. Now if you have to deal with location, product production, and/or employees this could take six to 18 months. The ultimate determination is your personal drive and will-power to achieve and meet goals.

Timeline 1:Example-Branding_____

Projected Dates:	Task(s):	Date Completed:
A.6.12.17_____	A.Have Logo Created _____	A.6.15.17_____
B.6.27.17_____	B.Have Flyer Created _____	B. 7.2.17_____
C.7.3.17_____	C.Create Social Media Page_____	C.7.2.17_____

Timeline 2: _____

Projected Dates:	Task(s):	Date Completed:
A._____	A._____	A._____
B._____	B._____	B._____
C._____	C._____	C._____
D._____	D._____	D._____

Timeline 3: _____

Projected Dates:	Task(s):	Date Completed:
A._____	A._____	A._____
B._____	B._____	B._____
C._____	C._____	C._____
D._____	D._____	D._____

Timeline 4: _____

Projected Dates:	Task(s):	Date Completed:
A._____	A._____	A._____
B._____	B._____	B._____
C._____	C._____	C._____
D._____	D._____	D._____

Timeline 5: _____

Projected Dates:	Task(s):	Date Completed:
A._____	A._____	A._____
B._____	B._____	B._____
C._____	C._____	C._____
D._____	D._____	D._____

Notes From Give Them The Business Podcast Episode #2

_____
_____
_____
_____
_____
_____
_____
_____
_____
_____
_____
_____
_____
_____
_____
_____
_____
_____
_____
_____
_____
_____
_____
_____

Exit 1 Examining the Map
Section 2
Identifying Your Target Market

Let's dig deeper into the who and what for your business, customers, and marketing.
The questions listed below you may not be able to answer in full detail now, but this page was designed for you to use annually or quarterly to review and revisit for your business's success. You need to know the answers to these questions and be able to answer when asked in any setting. This could be the difference between someone becoming an investor or not.

My Business

1) Who are we and what do we have to offer? _____
_____
_____
_____

2) What sets me apart from my competitors? _____
_____
_____
_____

3) What are my business goals for the upcoming year? _____
_____
_____
_____
_____

My Customers

4) Who is my target customer? _____
_____
_____
_____

5) What do my customers like best about my business? _____
_____
_____
_____

Exit 1 Examining the Map
Section 2
Identifying Your Target Market

6)   Where can I reach my target customers? _____
_____
_____
_____

My Marketing Plan

7)   What marketing activities have been successful for me in the past that I would like to continue? _____
_____
_____
_____

8)   What new online marketing activities would I like to tackle this year? _____
_____
_____
_____

9)   What new on-the-ground marketing activities would I like to tackle this year?

_____
_____
_____
_____

10)   What is my monthly marketing budget?

_____
_____
_____
_____

Notes From Give Them The Business Podcast Episode #3

PUTTING IN THE ADDRESS TO YOUR DESTINATION

Exit 2 Putting in the Address to Your Destination

Create a Vision and Mission Statement
Communicate a clear vision and purpose for your business

Vision Statement: A company's roadmap indicating what the company wants to become or it describes the clear and inspirational long-term desired growth resulting from organization, programs or work.
· The best statements are clear and precise.

Here are a few examples:
Feeding America: A hunger-Free America (Four words)
Alzheimer's Association: A World Without Alzheimer's
Make A Wish: That People Everywhere will share the power of a wish

Stop Here and Create a Visions Statement:

_____
_____
_____
_____
_____

Mission Statement: A written statement of an organization's core purpose and focus that normally remains unchanged over time.

AARP: To enhance quality of life for all as we age. We lead positive social change and deliver value to members through information, advocacy and service.

Make-A-Wish: We grant the wishes of children with life-threatening medical conditions to enrich the human experience with hope, strength and joy

Public Broadcasting System: To create content that educates, informs and inspires.
Stop here and create a mission statement:

_____
_____
_____
_____
_____

Exit 2 Putting in the Address to Your Destination

Elevator Speech: A brief speech that outlines an idea for a product or brief speech about your business. The name comes from the notion of the speech being delivered in the short time of an elevator ride.

Imagine this, you are attending networking event to meet potential clients and someone asked what do you do? Don't panic! Your elevator pitch will protect you! Practice your elevator speech just as you would free throws if you were in the NBA. Every time you add something new to your business you might want to think about adding it to your elevator speech as well.

Example Elevator Speech for a Business Lawyer:
"Hi! My name is Danny Waters and I'm a Business Lawyer at Trial Kings. I protect business's intellectual property and keep them out of court. I also work to create non-compete and non-disclosure agreements to protect his business. Do you know of anything I could help your business with?"

Example Personal Statement for a Financial Advisor:
"I'm a Financial Advisor at Advice Money I do free in-home consultations to look over your finances and come up with plans to get things back on track. A great referral for me is someone who's having trouble paying their monthly bills cause I know I can help. Do you or someone you know can use my services? Here are a couple of business cards for you."

Sample Elevator Speech for an Interior Designer Specialist:
"I work with people who are renovating their bathrooms and kitchens. When trying to sell a house these are the most important areas of a house. Whether you're selling or buying I can make your dream come true bathroom or kitchen. Don't forget to checkout the website on the card."

Example of an Elevator Speech for a Project Manager and Virtual Assistant:
"I own Big Fish Management where we manage projects so you don't have to. I fry the little fish so you can focus on the big fish. There are some task a CEO just shouldn't have to do. We organize your task and complete them on time or your money back. I'm sure there are some task I can help you with Mr. or Mrs. CEO."

Elevator Pitch Template for a Brand Developer:
"I own Visions Made Plain, a multimedia firm. Instead of companies hiring inexperienced help with their multimedia needs we fill that gap without the cost or overhead of an employee saving them both time and money. We specialize in graphics, photography, videography, social media marketing, web development, and branding campaigns. We build custom packages for any company at any level of business. Let's talk about how we can help your business.

Exit 2 Putting in the Address to Your Destination

Your Elevator Pitch will change as you grow. Let's track that growth here.

Write out your Elevator Speech:

_____
_____
_____
_____
_____
_____
_____
_____
_____
_____

Date_____

Write out your Elevator Speech after compeleting the workbook:

_____
_____
_____
_____
_____
_____
_____
_____
_____

Date_____

Write out your Elevator Speech 6 months later:

_____
_____
_____
_____
_____
_____
_____
_____
_____

Date_____

Notes From Give Them The Business Podcast Episode #4

_____

_____

_____

_____

_____

_____

_____

_____

_____

_____

_____

_____

_____

_____

_____

_____

_____

_____

_____

_____

_____

_____

_____

_____

_____

_____

_____

_____

Exit 3 Identifying The Business Structure

*Business Name
When creating a business name, make sure it isn't confusing to understand the type of business that it is. A sign with the name "George" and nothing else can be confusing. Is it George's Chicken and Waffles or, George Day Spa?

*Business Name
-Check to see if a business name is available before you start marketing it
-This is normally done by checking with your local Secretary of State
-Google it to see who has the name or one that is similar
-Is the domain name or something similar available?

*DBA (Doing Business As)
This name is sometimes requires in certain states and is considered fictitious business name, filings to be made for the protection of consumers conducting business with the entity. A company is said to be "doing business as" when the name under which they operate their business differs from its legal register name.

Decide on a Business Structure

What type of business structure will you be using? Select an option below that describes your business model.

Sole-Proprietor- A business that legally has no separate existence from its owner. The sole proprietor is the simplest business form under which one is operated. As a business owner, you are personally responsible for all business debts.

Partnership-The state of being a partner or partners. An association of two or more. Corporation- Prospective shareholders exchange money, property, or both, for the corporation's capital stock. A corporation generally takes the same deductions as a sole proprietor to figure it's tax deductible. A corporation can take special deductions.

S Corporation- Corporations that elect pass corporate income, losses, deductions, and credits through their shareholders for federal tax purposes. Shareholders of S corporations report the flow-through of income and losses on their personal tax return and are assessed tax at their individual income tax rates.
*Irs.gov has more detailed information

LLC-A corporate structure whereby the member of the company cannot be held personally liable for company's debts or liabilities. "LLC" is a separate and distinct legal entity. This means that an LLC can obtain a tax identification number, open a bank account a do business, all under its own name. (Highly recommended)

Exit 3 Identifying The Business Structure

Federal Tax Obligations- the tax you pay to the IRS, is determined by the form of business entity that you establish. These taxes include:

Income Tax- All businesses except partnerships must file an annual income tax return. The form you use is depending on your business organizational structure. Refer to Publication 583 for more information...

Self-employment Tax- Self employed tax is a social security and Medicare tax primarily for individuals that work for themselves.

Estimated Taxes- You must pay taxes on income, including self employment taxes by making regular payments or estimated payments to the IRS.

Employer Tax- When you have employees, you as the employer have certain taxes you must pay and are responsible for and forms you must file.

Excise tax- see irs.gov or sba.com

Notes From Give Them The Business Podcast Episode #5

_____
_____
_____
_____
_____
_____
_____
_____
_____
_____
_____
_____
_____
_____
_____
_____
_____
_____
_____
_____
_____
_____
_____
_____

Exit 4 Get off at the Rest Stop
Let's Do a Quick Analysis before we start that business plan

S.W.O.T Analysis

Strengths
We provide event planning
We share expenses

Weaknesses
We don't have any start up cash
We all have our hands in many other projects

Opportunities
We go in with a large amount of leads because there's four of us
We share the workload

Threats
Free programs that provide similar services
Not having a building with a sign to let people know where we are located yet

Let's Create a SWOT Analysis for your business:

Strengths
_____
_____
_____

Weaknesses
_____
_____
_____

Opportunities
_____
_____
_____

Threats
_____
_____
_____

Create a SWOT Analysis of your competitors

Strengths
_____
_____
_____

Weaknesses
_____
_____
_____

Opportunities
_____
_____
_____

Threats
_____
_____
_____

Notes From Give Them The Business Podcast Episode #6

_____

_____

_____

_____

_____

_____

_____

_____

_____

_____

_____

_____

_____

_____

_____

_____

_____

_____

_____

_____

_____

_____

_____

_____

Exit 5 Prepare for the Rest of the Trip
Basic Business Summary Outline

Before we get back out on the road to finish our journey, some things should be completed by now. Some questions will be familiar, but you should have some adjustments to them at this stage of the trip. This is where you can make a detour. That highway may have looked good when no ones else was on it, but now it looks like 5 o'clock traffic. Do you need to change your route? If so, why? _____

_____

_____

_____

Or is the same route still the best route? If so, why? What information did your research provide? _____

_____

_____

_____

Executive Summary:
This is a snapshot of your business plan as a whole and touches on your company profile and goals.
List yours here:

_____

_____

_____

Company Description:
This provides the description on what you do, the market your business serves, and what makes your business stand out from others.
Write yours below:

_____

_____

_____

Company Mission Statement:
A written statement of an organization's core purpose and focus that normally remains unchanged over time.
Write yours below:

_____

_____

_____

Exit 5 Prepare for the Rest of the Trip
Basic Business Summary Outline

Company Vision Statement:
A vision statement is a company's roadmap indicating what the company wants to become or it describes the clear and inspirational long-term desired growth resulting from organization, programs or work..

Write yours below:
_____
_____
_____

Brand Promise Statement:
A strong brand promise is one that connects your purpose, positioning, strategy, people and customer experience. It enables you to deliver your brand in a way that connects emotionally with your customers and differentiates your brand "from others".
Write yours out:
_____
_____
_____

Market Analysis:
A market analysis is a quantitative and qualitative assessment of a market. It looks into the size of the market both in volume and value, the various customer segments and buying patterns, the competition, and the economic environment in terms of barriers to entry and regulation.
Based from your research, what is your business industry, competitors, and the market you plan to serve in
Write yours below:
_____
_____
_____

Organizational Structure:
An organizational structure defines how activities such as task allocation, coordination and supervision are directed toward the achievement of organizational aims. Organizational structure can also be considered as the viewing glass or perspective through which individuals see their organization and its environment.

What's the best structure for your business? Every business has a different structure.
Write yours below:
_____
_____
_____

Exit 5 Prepare for the Rest of the Trip
Basic Business Summary Outline

Line of Business/ Service or Product Line

A LOB (line-of-business) is a general term that describes the products or services offered by a business or manufacturer. A company that manufactures solid state disk drives, for example, might claim their LOB is data storage.
What do you offer and sell? How does it benefit your customers? How will you sell your product or service?

_____
_____
_____

Marketing & Sales
What is your marketing plan or strategy? What is your sales strategy?
Short Term 1-5yr _____

_____
_____
_____

Long Term 5-10yr

_____
_____
_____

Funding Request
How will your business be funded?

_____
_____
_____

Financial Projections
Provide financial projections.

_____
_____
_____
_____

Appendix
An appendix is an optional, but useful place to include resumes, permits, and leases. List the types needed for your business:

_____
_____
_____

Notes From Give Them The Business Podcast Episode #7

_____

_____

_____

_____

_____

_____

_____

_____

_____

_____

_____

_____

_____

_____

_____

_____

_____

_____

_____

_____

_____

_____

_____

Exit 6 Taking a Stop to Tour the Land

Questions on the Tour:

Are you providing a product, service or both?

_____
_____
_____

What do you offer and/or sell?

_____
_____
_____

How does it benefit your customers?

_____
_____
_____

How will you sell your product or service?

_____
_____
_____

What does a similar business sale and how is yours different? What is the future direction of your business?

_____
_____
_____

How scalable is your business?

_____
_____
_____

How is your business helping the community or solving a problem? _____

_____
_____
_____

What is your marketing plan or strategy? What is your sales strategy?

_____
_____
_____

Notes From Give Them The Business Podcast Episode #8

_____

_____

_____

_____

_____

_____

_____

_____

_____

_____

_____

_____

_____

_____

_____

_____

_____

_____

_____

_____

_____

_____

_____

_____

_____

_____

28

Exit 7 Creating an itinerary for your day-to-day activities

Let's Create a timeline to a business launch
Below is an example of a simple timeline:

Launch Plans:
Make Business Legal
Get logo design
Start social media/web
Secure Location/ Make Flyer Launch party

Date
Week 1 August
I did _____

_____

Week 2
I did _____

_____

Week 3
I did _____

_____

Week 4
I did _____

_____

Weekly Hours to work my business
5pm-7pm I did _____
_pm-_pm I did _____
_pm-_pm I did _____
_pm-_pm I did _____
_pm-_pm I did _____

This plan above was designed with a person who is trying to fire their boss to become a full-time entrepreneur. Notice that this involves late working hours. If you don't have a full-time job, your hours should be increased.

Exit 7 Creating an itinerary for your day-to-day activities

Point to Ponder: In order to fire your day job, you have to give your own business time daily.

Other things to consider adding in your timeline:
The number represent the average cost per line item

1)   Logo 150

2)   Photography session (headshots, product shots, promo/stock images) 150

3)   Business Cards 150

4)   Flyers/Promotional Designs 150

5)   Social Media Professional Pages & Covers 75

6)   Website Development 600

7)   Brochure/ Newsletter 150

8)   Video Tour (if Brick and Mortar) 150

9)   Introductory Commercial 450

10)   Promotional Commercial 450

Monthly Budget Example:
$125 have a18-24 month plan
$250 have a 9-12 month plan
$500 have a 4-6 month plan
$1000 have a 2-3 month plan

These are just estimates to help you create a budget for the cost of these different items. Pricing information from Visionsmadeplain.com

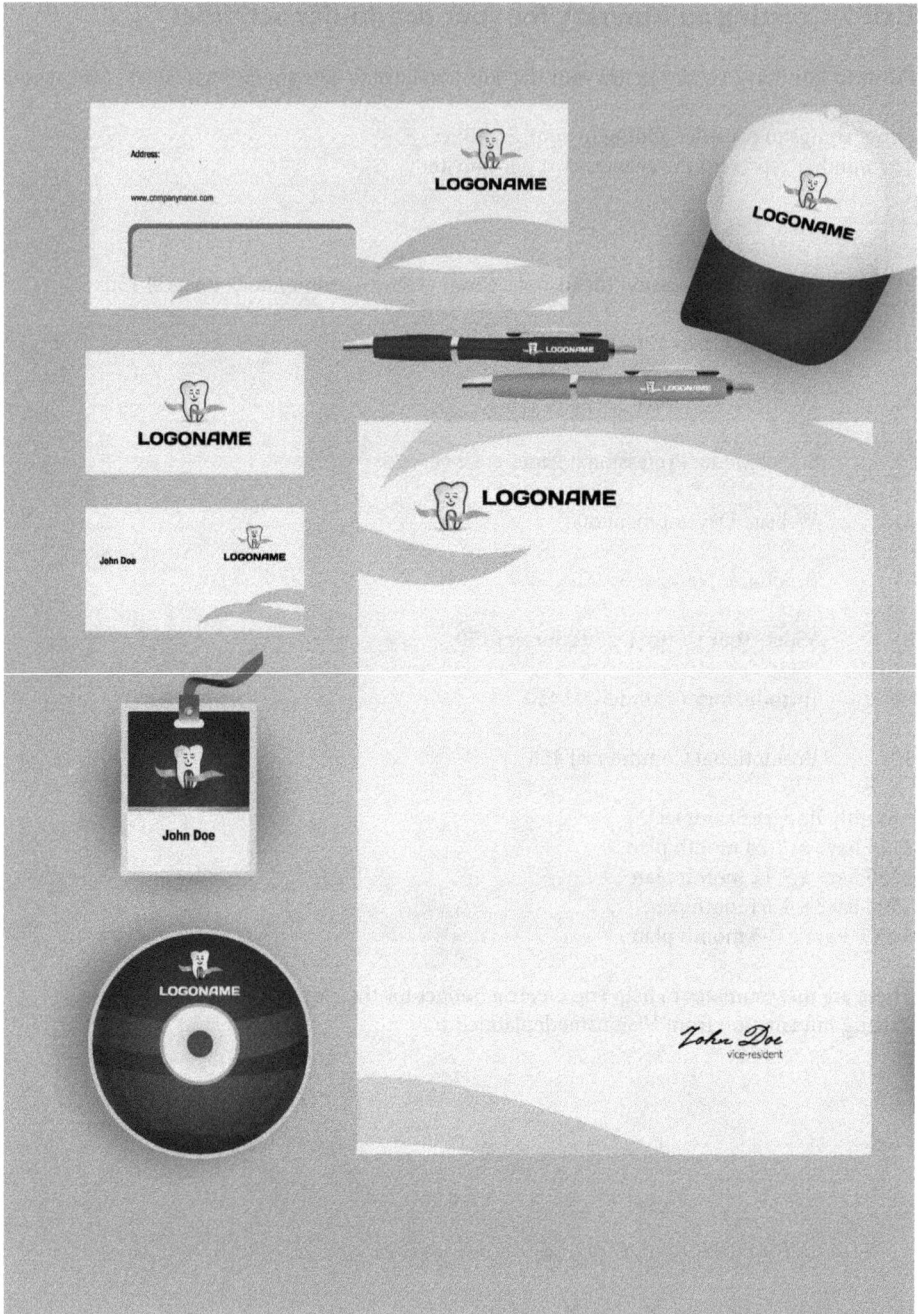

Notes From Give Them The Business Podcast Episode #9

Exit 8 Let's talk Legal

*Insurance -a practice or arrangement by which a company or government agency provides a guarantee of compensation for specified loss, damage, illness, or death in return for payment of a premium.

*Check with local insurance companies that offer business insurance. Your car insurance provider can be a start.
*Legal legalshield.com is a good way to start having a legal team on your side.

*Confidentiality Policy -a policy put in place for the protection of personal information. Confidentiality means keeping a client's information between you and them, and not telling others including co-workers, friends, and family.

*Copyright -the exclusive legal right, given to an originator or an assignee to print, publish, perform, film, or record literary, artistic, or musical material, and to authorize others to do the same.

*Patents -a government authority or license conferring a right or title for a set period, especially the sole right to exclude others from making, using, or selling an invention.

Steps to Making Legal:

-Do all the homework this book requires

-Get your EIN irs.gov

-Register Your Name (This is normally done with your county clerk office or with your state government, depending on where your business is located).

-Do Business Structure Paperwork

-Get Your Business License

-Contact Your local SBA (they provide free counseling, and business assistance)

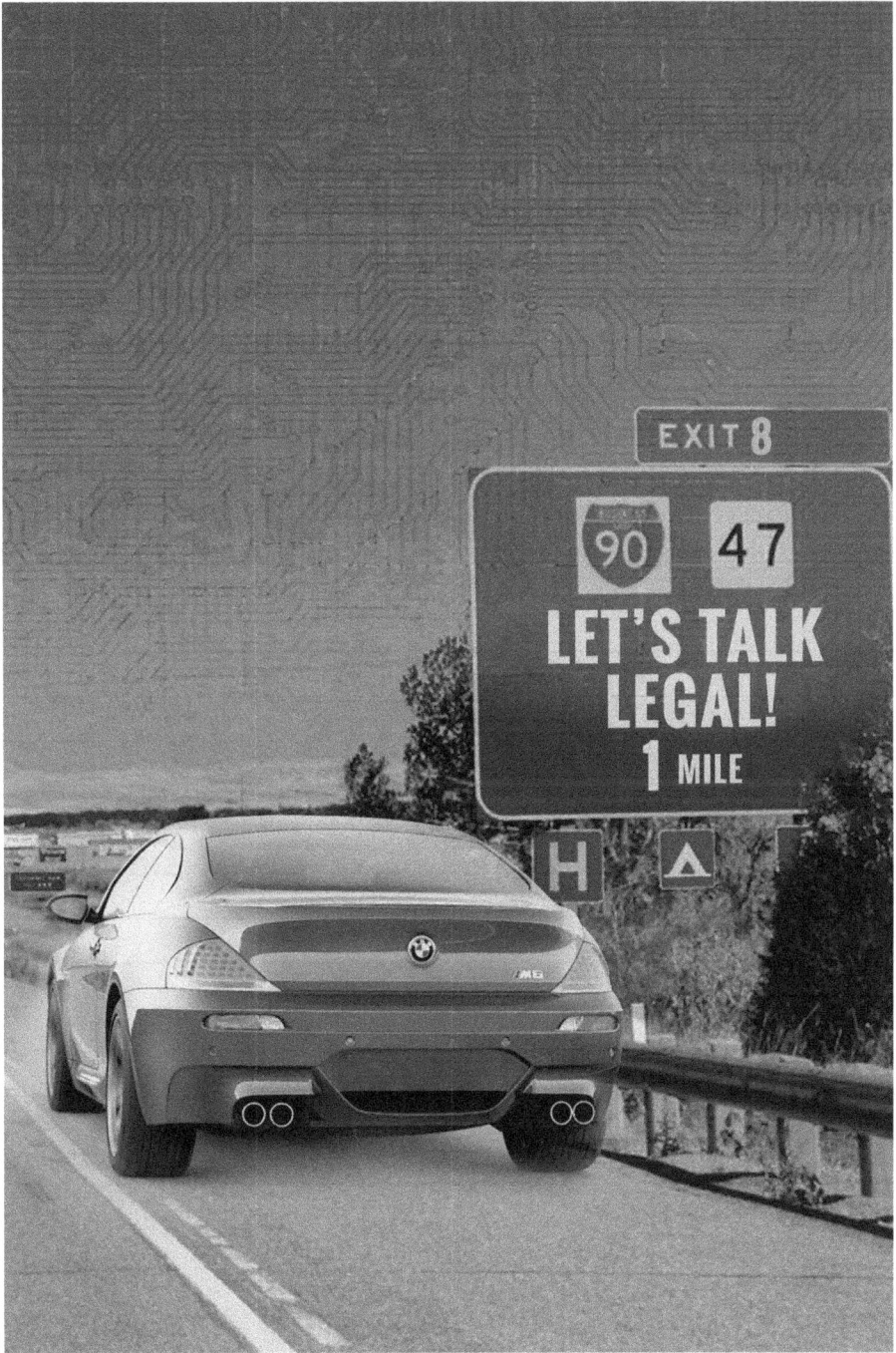

Notes From Give Them The Business Podcast Episode #10

Exit 9 Delegating Different Drivers

Define what is needed to make your business grow. Determine the type of diversity you would like on your team. (Intern, Professional, Diverse, or Mothers) this will be based on your business model/plan. What position is needed on your team for what you will need in 1 year, 5 years, or 10 years? Start looking at the type of people who fit into your team's building plan.

*Create what would be the expectation of the team members you want.
*Make sure you have a manual in place with the day-to-day operations of your business.

Team Member 1 (Example)
Secretary

Daily Job Task:

-Answer calls

-File papers

-Post on social media

-Respond to emails and messages

-Confirm appointments

-Schedule new appointments

-Send invoices

*Build your team from the top down to ensure that every function of your business is taken care of.

*Create your business from day one and how you want it to look year one. (Flip back to your vision statement)

Exit 9 Delegating Different Drivers

Stop Here and Take a Coffee Break from Driving
Let's create your ideal team members:

Team Member #1

_____
_____
_____
_____
_____
_____
_____
_____
_____
_____

Team Member #2

_____
_____
_____
_____
_____
_____
_____
_____
_____
_____

Team Member #3

_____
_____
_____
_____
_____
_____
_____
_____
_____
_____

Notes From Give Them The Business Podcast Episode #11

_____
_____
_____
_____
_____
_____
_____
_____
_____
_____
_____
_____
_____
_____
_____
_____
_____
_____
_____
_____
_____
_____
_____
_____
_____
_____

Exit 10 You Have Arrived at Your Destination

You looked around in your hotel room, it's beautiful and now you get to enjoy all of your hard work.

-You look at all the beautiful manuals created

-Your Business Plan

-Your legal documents

-Keep in mind, you are going to always make changes to your business plan and polish things along the way.

TIME TO CELEBRATE!

Tips for your journey (when you get tired because you will get tired):

-Relax, meditate, and most importantly pray

-Review Exits 1 & 2

-Refer Back to your Why

-Build multiples teams/people

-Take failures as a lessons and move on in your journey.

Basic Business Plan Outline Checklist

~Business Structure

__**Title Page** Your Company's Name, Address, Phone, Fax, Email, and Website
__**Non-Disclosure** May be needed if plan is to show others
__**Brand Promise** (Your mission and vision)
__ **Executive Summary** 1-3 pages that highlight your business concept (sales pitch)
__**Company Description** (A description solving the problem your customers have)
__**Operations/Your Solution** (Your product or service)
__**Business Model** (How you make money)
__**Management Team** Describe each manager experience and expertise and include what their job description would be

~Marketing

__**Target Market** (who is your customer and why)
__**Competitive Advantage** (Pull things from SWOT analysis to help determine your unique competitive advantages)

~Financial Plan

__**Projected Profit and Expenses**
__**Cash Flow Tables**
__**Business Monthly Budget (Cost of doing business)**
__**Determine Insurance Needs**

~Other
__**Hire,** on a per hour basis an accountant or lawyer
__**Hire,** on a per hour basis bookkeeper or tax professional

Top Ten Business Tips

-Pay God, yourself, taxes and your bills

-Account for every penny

-Keep a paper trail for every portion of your business

-Shortcuts limit experience

-Take your time and do it right the first time

-Create a marketing budget early on

-Develop your team create standard operating procedures

-Educate yourself daily on your industry

-Great planning from the beginning saves you time in the end

-Always create an exit plan before starting

Notes From Give Them The Business Podcast Episode #12

About the Authors

Joy McLaughlin-Harris is from Gadsden, SC. She is a leadership educator, speaker, and author. Her organizations have trained thousands of leaders on personal development, business development, and financial literacy. Joy McLaughlin-Harris is the founder of Touch of Joy, a non-profit organization and CEO of Verve Salon Suites. Every year, she speaks to groups, provides seminars, and host events to promote leadership, financial literacy, and business development. She has appeared on television as an awesome business woman, leadership coach, and entrepreneur.

Touch of Joy International
1-800-570-3544
www.touchofjoy.org
PO box 23334
Columbia, SC 29224

Daryn Murphy is from Columbia, SC. He started his first business at the age of 13. He had started three businesses while in middle school and has been an entrepreneur on some scale ever since. His focus is to empower and equip as many people as possible with business savvy. He has worked with over a thousand business owners in brand development, business development, business structuring, and marketing strategies. He believes that everybody has a business within them just waiting to come out. Daryn is the CEO of Visions Made Plain LLC, a multimedia firm where he helps people develop their business brand, structure income streams, and marketing in this new digital world. He also owns Studio Arts, a digital media production house studio specializing in live streaming , podcasts, and video productions.

Visions Made Plain
803-250-6185
visionsmadeplain.com
106 Quinton Ln.
Columbia, SC 29229

www.ingramcontent.com/pod-product-compliance
Lightning Source LLC
Chambersburg PA
CBHW071126210326
41519CB00020B/6433